THE MAJESTIC CEMETERY'S GUIDE TO

FIND YOUR FANTASTIC™

One Man's Journey through Transition and Adversity

to Find Meaning and Purpose in Life

BY

MARCEA WEISS

Calypso Publishing

Digital ISBN 978-0-9912663-0-2

Print ISBN 978-0-9912663-1-9

First Edition

February 2014

Foreword:

It was late in the year, as playing outside no longer held the desire that it had in the past. As a child, my mind was not clouded, but simple. All that I could think of was playing- the toys that were fun and the sisters that I loved to play with. For many reasons, not only the amount of work required on our Dairy Farm, I never found enough hours in the day to bring together the sisters and toys or time to play.

I remember the moment when the solution came to me as a young child of about four. It was not something that I tried to hide from my parents. That thought never occurred to me, but also was not about to waste their time with it either. Simply, I decided the best solution was to get up in the middle of the night, ask my sisters to join me and find additional (and much needed, in my view) time to play.

The plan worked great for a while. It all came together and I remember a certain sense of accomplishment, as much as one can have when still living in the age of single digits, for making this happen. The scene was this- one of my sisters and I in the living room, toys a plenty, playing together in the middle of the night. That was until, Mom discovered us, somewhat surprised, and ushered us back to bed.

This memory has come back to me over the past few years as a guiding light. When you find something or the things that you like to do and are good at, you will without hesitation spend all hours of the day and night engaged in them.

I have wondered why we lose this singular focus. How can we avoid this and bring as much as possible of it back into our lives, without the necessity of moving back into our parents' homes?!

It seems that we spend much of our young adult lives learning to face reality; working to be realistic. During this time, many of us lose the connection with our deepest desires, joys and passions. We lose the connection to our inner self, our soul and in my mind our real purpose for being here in the first place.

How wonderful this life and world will be when we are all able to keep the simple-ness and clarity of thought carried over from childhood- less analysis, less factoring in past failures, less doubt and worry about the future, more faith, joy and love.

How can we accomplish this? I believe that many of us do. Some of us figure it out peacefully. Others put up a good fight, working to entrench ourselves in the daily grind and our devotion to reality until we realize that another options exists.

Let's read through a story of one young man and his journey through this discovery...

Chapter One
A wise man comes to town.

As the shadows moved from one side of the tree to the other and the Spring sunshine began to warm the air, the streets could best be described as inactive. A lack of movement. A lack of sound. A lack of people.

This was a great metaphor for his life over the past few days and weeks, Melk thought. When was the last time he had engaged in a substantial conversation? What was it about? What of significance did his mind carry right now? He had tried a few days back, stopping in a café for a quick and economical meal. The waitress, he remembered, seemed so pleasant, so "in the moment" and really interested in the conversation.

The only problem, Melk recalled was that he had no conversation. Even up until the present time, he felt as if he had nothing on his mind, and at the same time, the whole world. He should have a lot on his mind shouldn't he? Shouldn't he have a lot to discuss? What a disconnection. That's a great summary, Melk realized. He felt disconnected.

He'd been in town only a few days, delayed by a local storm system that had slowed him down on his progress as he drove toward the east. Heading somewhere, but not really anywhere.

Then, it had happened. He was not sure if it had been a nail or wear over time. He was not sure of what exactly pierced his tire, but it had done an effective job. Drive train damage was not something that he had been expecting, not usually a part of a simple flat tire. His bank account clearly told that he was not expecting the bill either.

Now, here he was in a new town, a town of strangers, not much unlike the last one really. In fact, he was not sure that it was a town of strangers, because not many faces had shown up since his arrival yesterday afternoon.

The one face that did stick in his mind was that of the auto attendant letting him know how much it would cost to get back on the road. He'd have to learn to love this town after all, at least for the near future.

It was one more bump in the road. The road had been a long one, starting thousands of miles away and working east over time. Along the route, he'd been enamored by many things- moving from one good job to another, from one home to another and even from one relationship to another. Each move seemed to make sense at the time, at times he felt on top of the world. Now, he wondered and reviewed in his mind again how it had all come down to this point- alone and financially broke in a strange town far away.

He had really been groomed to think and strive for the best. He believed in having a vision and working toward his goals or he had any way. He cared about efficiency. His time in competitive sports had done a lot to drive these desires. Melk knew that hard work paid off and that the force of good does prevail in the long run. Faith was a big part of his life.

Still, it had been a long time since he had been able to settle down and stay on one course without an impending move or shifting focus. This was not true in Melk's youth. He had a stable childhood, perhaps too stable really. Good family, available to him in a safe environment.

Was it this environment that launched him into the world at one hundred miles an hour at his first effort? Some of it was a blur now. He remembered a strong desire to get out and see the world beyond the west coast boundaries, beyond the limits he'd known growing up.

Melk was short for Melkior a name of old, one of the three wise men from biblical times. This had intrigued him as a child, bringing him visions of grandeur, believing he was destined for greatness, inspiring him to have great ideas and beliefs that he could accomplish anything and fostering his desires to do so.

Yes, those were good days, Melk thought. The days when he ignored or was not yet aware of reality and felt anything was possible. Then, as he grew older, he had experienced a taste, or even a few tastes- Some would say more than his fair share of tastes- of success. He had chased them and tried to "follow his star." Wasn't that our mission after all? Wasn't that what he had been trained to do?

His current perspective led him to believe that this had been a lost cause. Melk was left questioning a lot of what he had previously believed. He found himself starting to yearn for more simplicity in his life.

Analysis had been a big part of his approach in the past. Numbers were his friend and he was proud of that. He had been proud to show off how he could form a calculated spreadsheet with loads of data to use in making the best decision. The numbers all started broadly at the top and in a detailed, well thought out fashion, led to the answer he'd been seeking near the end.

He had to ask how far this approach had brought him. A sure sign of the need to try a new approach. Simplicity was working for him these days. The solution to finding a new place to stay and a way to pay for transportation was clearly the best place to start. The simple approach, in many ways seemed refreshing.

Hadn't he seen many people through the years that lived in this manner? They did not analyze every step or desire to continuously improve. They seemed and looked happy. Maybe their burden was reduced? On the outside, he had seen, these people, manning the tolls, mowing the lawns, organizing the books and in many ways looking the same as he. They shared the same physiology, same psychology, he thought and appeared satisfied.

He had always drawn a line between himself and this group. In wonderment, he had felt that their lives would not be the right fit for him. He just could not do that. He could not and prided himself in the realization that he did not want to just lock into autopilot and coast along.

Now, his desires and ambitions and yes impatience had led him to this place where he envied these others. They looked more comfortable than ever right now in comparison to his situation. Well, when the shoe fits, he thought...

Perhaps, he had been blinded by youthful ambition at the time? He remembered others suggesting this to him. New initiatives that he'd try to lead, new efforts that fought the status quo were many times met with the same responses. "We've tried that.. Someone tried that.. They were smarter than you, taller than you, better looking than you and it didn't work..." The comments usually included a prediction or desire, really, he thought, that one day he would slow down, he would blend in, he would back off and join the ranks versus his continuous focus on moving forward, acceleration and taking the next step.

How had this come to be? He had always known that as much as he enjoyed his team mates and coworkers and family members, his allegiance was to "true north," he thought. He really wanted to be true to himself. He had worked hard to get to the point where he'd arrived- youth sports and activities, college, national level sports and more. He'd made a continuous effort to distinguish himself and it had worked. So, if his work made people uncomfortable, pushed them to do more, more than encouraged them to leave their comfort zone, he just could not apologize. He should not have to, should he?

First, it was the job. The first job. What once had been so great, where he had quickly set achievement records, now had reversed. It seemed that some had resented or not settled well to his approach. Maybe he did not follow the system as well as he should have? As well as they did?

Then, again, his next challenge came quickly and he jumped at it with great motivation as he had in the past, with the same head turning result. He found himself on the 'get it done' list of many of the higher leaders and then, later, the 'get it gone' list of other leaders. He remembered his goal had not been to blend in, but maybe in the end, he had stuck too far out?

When the economy slowed, Melk had found himself in a pinch. It was not a great time to be out looking for a job, and yet, here he was. And he was looking. He had been looking for over a year. He never planned to make this town of Majestic home.

Underneath all of this, Melk knew it would come to a head. He believed that it had to. Good is more powerful than evil and he was here to be a positive force in the world. He would be offered that opportunity, wouldn't he? He believed so and really hoped his faith could hold out long enough to realize it.

While he was in the auto garage, Melk asked for advice on finding a job. He was straight forward in letting them know that repayment would happen for sure, but not with his current resources. He'd have to find local work to satisfy the bill. He'd asked for their advice on this matter. They did not have much to say. It seemed as if everyone working there in the shop had been there for quite some time. Job searching had not been a concern of theirs in any memorable past. So, he'd head out and be on his own in this new town, searching for employment and housing, on foot nonetheless.

One of the workers at the garage did send him in the direction of lodging, down the road, shared quarters near what must have been the downtown area. Anywhere else in Melk's past and it would have been considered very rural, but in Majestic it was downtown. Melk stopped in and found a room.

Before his car broke down, Melk had been traveling for quite some time, arriving from far away. He hoped this would be his last move. He had changed jobs and friends many times. He wondered about purpose and wandered looking for a goal and for a future plan. He felt as if he was in a hurry, but not sure of the final destination. He had not expected to spend so much time here in this town.

It seemed a beautiful town, or one that could be. Near a great body of water with clear air, he had thought it might have been a place that in another time, he may have included on one of his outings, but not like this. He had better get back on task, Melk thought.

Sometimes it felt to Melk as if he was living outside of his own skin, living someone else's life. He could remember a time for him, not too long ago when things were very different. He worked, he shopped, he socialized and he had goals. Now, so much time was spent thinking about now, about getting through today. It was very different.

In this new town, things did not happen as quickly as he hoped. People did not respond. The answer did not arrive. He had no job. He had found housing. This was progress, he tried to assure himself.

He walked to clear his head past a posting on a fence,

**Help needed: Mowing, trimming, and
equipment operation.
Apply within.**

He had almost not noticed as he was heavy in thought thinking of nothing. This was not what he was seeking, was it? Melk spoke to himself. How could it not be? Wasn't he just describing his willingness or desire to join the simple life, the satisfied workers, to be open to something new? Maybe what he had been thinking was that what mattered was finding something and he should not and could not be picky.

As Melk walked and thought, he stopped to check in at the garage to see how the repairs were progressing. The repairs continued to move slowly and mount in cost. Melk knew that finding a job would be the only way to get moving again.

While there, he mentioned the posting of the cemetery job opening that he'd seen. The man behind the service station counter had been there for some time. He had no problem sharing history of neighbors or local families or even history and stories of this historic town. He had done so.

However, at the mention of the cemetery, he slowed down. He seemed to not have much to say, cocked his head back, closed his eyes and shook his head, curling up his face. Really, I've not heard much. As he said this, he looked at Melk. "You don't take me as a cemetery worker, do you?" the man asked.

The name on the fence sign read, "Majestic Cemetery." It was nestled on a rise above the great body of water. Melk could just make out the tail end of a fading rainbow overhead. Remarkable. When was the last time he had seen one of these- a cemetery or a rainbow? He could not recall.

Melk suddenly remembered the comments of the service station worker asking if he looked like a cemetery worker. Melk thought, "Do I?" Melk reassured himself by saying "Surely, he must be here for a reason, whatever that means." Melk almost laughed. What was he talking about? He wasn't any kind of worker. He was unemployed and allowing his mind to get very far ahead of himself and reminded himself he must keep moving.

Melk walked through the front gate of the cemetery discontinuing his thoughts and was caught by a damp clear breeze and fresh air. When was the last time that he'd been to a cemetery, he wondered? It was peaceful, rigid and beautiful. It was also unsettling in a way. He was not sure what way, but he felt it. He walked further.

As a youth, Melk remembered the loss of his pet, then the loss of his grandparents. It was intense. It was sad, and then it was over. He remembered blurred weekends and grieving relatives at his grand parents' funerals. Stories were shared. It had been sad and many were upset, he recalled. Then, life had gone on. He had not spent much time since then thinking about cemeteries or death; I guess you would call it, to be more specific.

"It's not what I need to be thinking now," Melk thought and he continued on. He was confident that he could pick up on the new work and his rural background would allow him to quickly learn and physically adjust to whatever tasks were required by the job.

A man in suspended overalls emerged from the office and greeted Melk, "Welcome to the Majestic Cemetery. Can I help you?"

"I've noticed that you are.. Are you looking for help?" Melk stammered.

"Yes," the man responded. "We are. We are looking for someone right away to help with grounds upkeep. Any experience in the past with landscaping or work in the field?"

Melk nodded and asked if he could complete an application for the work. The man introduced himself as Bob, the Superintendent and gave Melk an application. Melk completed it and returned it.

"I have to ask," Melk said. "The application says 1 week employment term. Is that correct?"

Bob nodded, "Yes, it is correct. We are offering a week of work. We need people who care about the work that they are doing. It is certainly not for everyone. It is tough work that requires a compassionate hand. Are you interested?"

"Yes, I'm interested, but one week seems strange. How can that be? Won't you need the help all year?"

"Yes," Bob said, "It's true that many find this to be unique. The truth is that we are unique. Everything that you'll need to know you will learn in one week. During the week, our work will be completed. Nothing lasts forever. Bob paused and then with an odd expression said, "Wouldn't that be unsettling if it did!"

Melk thought to himself that of all things he'd learned, he'd discovered that statement the hard way. What had he experienced in his life that had lasted forever? He had a hard time working out an answer to this. Then, Melk remembered, "I need to keep myself on task here. One week would work if that was the need. It would be one week more than what was on his calendar currently."

That night, Melk spent some time thinking about this plan and the day that had passed. He had never expected a cemetery, but he was relieved to find the job. It was what he'd needed for a while now. He thought more about expectations and surprises and guarantees. He'd had surprises in his life and knew to keep moving forward when they arrived, not to panic, you might say. In fact, many times Melk thought, things had turned out better than what he had expected. He had always been a "thinker" he'd been told and he'd noticed it in his life.

First, starting out, Melk had set goals, he was looking for technical work in computers and had the training to support it. He found the work and enjoyed it for a certain amount of time. Then, things changed. The employment changed and he found himself in a different line of work that had not been on "the list." He found it was better, more rewarding and enjoyable. He had learned at this moment that he should be careful what he hoped for. In some cases, Melk thought, he might have been the worst at mapping out the best future for himself.

These thoughts had crossed Melk's mind in the past. He'd explored them, but being the logical person that he prided himself to be, it did not quite connect. It did not quite make sense. If he was not the one to build the strategy and course for his life, then who was? Was he meant to just "go with the flow" and allow fate to take over? Melk could not believe that either. He had certainly seen the value of hard work, vision and persistence in his life.

Still, to this day, Melk felt proud of his ability to work hard, something he had learned outdoors as he was growing up and it had served him well, both professionally and personally.

Well, if hard work pays off, yet the path never stretches out in front of me in the exact manner that I had planned, how do I move forward in this life, Melk reasoned. Simple came back to his mind. Perhaps, he need not derive this answer tonight. Perhaps, tonight, he could celebrate the small step of solving the initial, immediate problem of employment. Perhaps, the intersection of hard work in the unexpected locale of a cemetery would serve him well again. He had stumbled up on his future as he'd done in the past and he could not help to feel some measure of excitement to see how it would turn out.

Melk arrived the next morning just after dawn. He mowed. He trimmed. His body ached almost immediately. He worked through it and wondered again about being there. As the day grew longer, his physical pain did too. He thought of his sports training and remember to coach himself to take it one day at a time.

Mostly, he wondered about the 1 week limit. "Surely," he thought, if I do a good job, I'll get extended to a more permanent role? Who knows really if I'll like it in the end," and he got back to work.

As Melk worked, he noticed how the landscape that had seemed so large at first now seemed to blend together. A continuous line seemed to blend between the stone monuments, his equipment and his body. The time ran together too and before he knew it, the sun began to set.

In the lowering light and the shifting colors, the cemetery was beautiful and the great body of water strong. The rainbow that had shone so brightly earlier in the day seemed to be flashing a fleeting goodbye in the colors of the sunset. Something twinkled near the end of the path. He moved closer and picked up the small **green** stone and read:

Use what you have. You have all that you need. Live in the present to see this.

"Strange," he thought. "Someone must have dropped this. I'll turn it into the office for anyone looking to find lost items."

He walked toward the office. Bob was seated and looked up from his work for a moment. "How's the day turning out?"

"It's fine. I think I'm getting the hang of things. I found a small rock with a printing on it, that I..."

Before Melk could continue, Bob cut him off, "We don't need extra rocks in the cemetery, especially small ones. As much as we can, we'll need you to collect anything like that that you see and remove it. The mowers are very capable of giving small items a mighty whack and sending them off in all sorts of damaging directions.

Thanks for your hard work today. We shall see you tomorrow. Rest up, you will need it."

With that, Bob was back to his work and Melk left to wrap up his first day. He spent time thinking about the message embedded in the rock. Maybe someone had misplaced it. He thought more and wondered. Is it possible that it was meant for him? He was open to any message that would help him work this way down his path of life. But, then again, maybe he was reading too much into this. He had to stay focused.

As he set the equipment back to its spot in the shed, he noticed an elderly woman nearby spending time at one of the grave sites. It was the first visitor that he'd noticed for the day. Were there others that he had not seen?

Melk thought about what a visitor meant, all that it represented. Her presence implied a loss. It represented a gap in her life, something missing, Melk thought. Was it still a fresh, raw grief? Melk did not think so. She seemed too at peace for that. She seemed to have herself together.

"Alright," Melk asked himself, "what did you expect?" He was back to his natural approach of working toward a logical proof. "If a cemetery implies loss and a visitor appears, she must be living with loss. If loss implies grief, she must be in pain."

In fact, she did not look in pain. She looked reflective. She looked quiet and peaceful, much like his first impression of the cemetery. Shouldn't I be able to see the loss and grief in her presence? Shouldn't I expect to see that here every day? Why did I not notice that when I first walked through the gate? Why is loss and grief not filling this environment? Why is it not filling every moment?

Melk realized what he had not thought before. He's trying to understand- to feel a feeling that was not familiar to him. He had not had great loss in his life. He'd realized that, but did not realize how much effort he had made to not think about it. It scared him.

Strange this was, he thought, for someone who prided himself on being logical, on being direct and straightforward. How, had he missed this reality in his life? How could it feel and appear so foreign to him?

If loss was loss, Melk thought, he had experienced that. He had lost a lot over the past few years. Key relationships, material items he had valued, stability, permanent location and more. He was not sure this was the same.

He realized that he had thought about it in the past. With the tragic deaths of world leaders and celebrities since his childhood, he had thought about it. National tragedies and dramatic media coverage had made him think about it briefly and then move on. Really, these experiences had pushed him further away from the concept of death rather than toward thinking about it, rather than facing his own eventual consequence.

They had pushed him to be sure that he was buried in his goals and his mission for whatever time that he had. It pushed him to work harder every day, to think more about his goals and to stretch to attain them. But, that's where it had stopped.

Strange, he thought. There is no doubt that one day I'll be here in one way or another. One day I'll be here visiting, grieving, living or not living with a loss. One day I'll be here in a different capacity. One day everyone will be. What will that be like?

Melk had attended Sunday school as a child. He believed and was full of faith. He knew that there was more after all of this, but had never connected the concepts in with his life, with his loss, with his future. That's where Melk, once again, thought about keeping it simple. He was not sure of the answer, but thought about what the right question might be. Yes, keep it simple.

What was simple? Simple was what would not get his mind circling in this fashion. It would allow him to know, as he had once as a child, what was important to him. To know, clearly what had to be done and what he wanted to do. In a way, he was lucky, his current circumstance made it easy to see what he had to do. He could stop the ongoing analysis and focus on the task at hand. Yes, that is simple and refreshing.

Melk had continued his walk from the shed, aware of the elderly lady as he moved closer and then past her section of the cemetery. As he stooped to remove trash that he'd noticed, she began to approach him.

"Pardon me, young man?"

"Yes, may I help you?" Melk responded.

"I just wanted to say hello. I have not seen you in the Majestic Cemetery in the past. I'm Sara and I visit the cemetery frequently since my late husband passed away unexpectedly."

"I'm sorry for your loss," Melk responded, trying to sound sincere.

"No need," Sara assured him. "My gain was far outweighed by my loss. However, I could have done better to see it coming. It should not have been a surprise and yet it was.

Well, probably enough on that. I wanted to welcome you and thank you for the hard work you are doing on the grounds. I really wanted to thank you."

"It is no problem. I am happy to be here," Melk responded. Was he really happy? Had he meant that?

Melk had not considered this part of the job when he started. Yes, he had realized that is was a cemetery, had not really thought about it. He was not sure that he wanted to hear about all this, but thought it important to be considerate and polite in his new position.

Sara took a break from telling her story and took a good look at Melk. "You don't look like any one that I've met in the cemetery before. This must be your first day. How are things going?"

"Well, everything is fine. I was looking for a job and now, I've found one. I think I've done a good job. Bob seems satisfied."

Sara looked more intently at Melk and asked, "Then, you are on the right track?"

"It's funny that you should ask that. It's something that I've thought a lot about these last few weeks while moving and searching for a job. Yes, I believe that I am." Her intense look was starting to make him uncomfortable.

"I want you to know something about this, The Majestic Cemetery. It is a place that is different. You may have noticed unique things today or extra-ordinary things. When this happens, I hope you'll take notice. I've ran into many people who have worked here in the past. Some have really taken note and changed their lives. Others leave the same as when they arrived. It is truly a Majestic place and I hope you'll take time to notice."

Melk felt the day growing longer and was not sure what to say. He felt Sara's intent gaze and stumbled through, "Yes, I'm certain that I will. Again, I'm sorry for your loss."

Sara smiled slightly and gave a slight brush to Melk's shoulder. "In the loss, can be found a great gift. It was true for me and I think, no, I hope that it will be true for you; that your losses will lead you to your greatest gifts as well."

Sara stretched as if preparing to move. She reached into her pocket and removed a folded piece of paper. "I'd like to share this with you. I hope you'll enjoy my notes."

Melk thanked Sara and put the paper into his pocket. He wished her a good night and wondered what she could possibly know about his loss. Was it written on his face? Should he consider any of his past a loss? Things had changed rapidly and unexpectedly. He had never expected to end up here in the Majestic Cemetery. He thought, I guess there is some loss. Did that mean there was grief also? Maybe the concept was not as foreign as he had thought. Either way, he was relieved that the conversation with Sara was over.

Melk closed up the remaining items in the shed, and made his way out of the cemetery, down the road to his home. During the trip, he was aware of the new items that had found him in his pocket.

It was a short walk home. Over dinner, he removed the stone that he'd found and the paper that Sara had given to him. He had felt too awkward to open it up or read it in the cemetery, but now, his curiosity got the best of him. He read the written words on the paper as he unfolded it.

> *Dear friend,*
>
> *I miss you. Our time together was not enough. I did not expect the direction that was given to us. I would like the time to do over again. I'd like to be able to tell myself that there is no time except for the right now. That is the time to live to the fullest, to enjoy to greatest extent.*
>
> *When we were together, I thought too much about what I wanted, what I needed, what would make me happy. I could not help but get caught up in thinking how the grass was or could be greener, or how it had been greener in other times. I missed much of our time together by doing this. I miss you and I treasure the memories, but I won't make that mistake again today.*
>
> *We certainly had our joyous times together and I treasure those. They brought us close together. I still laugh over the memories, you know? I wonder how many more we would have had, had we focused on the moments that we had in front of us, vs. planning for and creating expectations for the future or reliving the past.*
>
> *What they say is true. Life brings mistakes. Mistakes build Experience. Experience brings wisdom. I can now see that I am alive right now. I have everything that I need. I am not*

being distracted by the search for perfect or the far off unknown on the horizon.

You were not perfect and neither was I. I would have liked to have been OK with this when we were together. Today, I am.

I want to make the most of all of the WHO, WHAT, WHEN's that I have in my life right now, focusing on the PRESENT. I have everything that I need. Thank you for delivering this message in the most unexpected manner possible.

I want to thank you dear friend. I love you. I miss you. I'll see you soon.

Sara

P.S. Should it have really been all that unexpected? Why did we never talk about what this would be like? We should have seen it coming and the joy and focus that it could have brought us earlier (and, yes, the joy that it brings me today).

Melk read through the note one more time and then looked back at the rock with the embedded message:

Use What You Have; You have what you need; Live in the present to see this.

He thought about what this could mean in his life. Sara's note connected with him. He thought of the relationships in his life, of the Who, What, When's and how easy it was for him to be critical, to look at them and desire more or to think of what was lacking with each. He was not expecting to see joy mentioned toward the end of the note. She had lost her loved one and mentioned joy as a result. How could this be?

Melk realized that he experienced what Sara was talking about. In many moments, he felt as if he was living in another time, or at least focusing on another time, the past or the present. He spent a lot of time thinking about what he would change in the past and trying to map out what he hoped for in the future. Every time he did this, he carried himself away from the present. In each of these instances, this deep thought tore him away from the only moment that really mattered- the only interactions and situations that he could really influence.

In the present, Melk realized, is where he was an active participant. In the past, he worked and re-worked his analysis of what was good, what was bad, what should have gone differently, been said differently and more. His thoughts of the future were very similar. He'd think about what he should say in certain situations, on which situation would be best to hope for, which would be best to expect. These were places where he had no influence.

Melk used his result-focused mind to really observe this condition. How had these focused, unending thoughts affected results or happiness in his life? Had they? Sure, he had looked at both the past and the future from all angles and even mapped out his preferred future, his dreams they had been called. And then, they worked out differently. They worked out on their own- usually for the better. He certainly had not asked for the car trouble and it led to this gainful employment.

Perhaps, he would spend less mental effort "time travelling" and more time in the present.

Melk remembered a phrase that he'd heard in the past, recounted it and agreed:

> **The past is history.**
> **The future is a mystery.**
> **The present is a gift.**

Did he truly have everything that he needed for right now? Maybe, the question, he thought was what did he really need right now? Was it better relationships? Was it more stuff? Was it fancier stuff? What was important to him?

Melk realized that he really wanted to be fulfilled. Yes, he'd have to pay his bills. He really appreciated the relationships in his life and it could be fun to purchase new toys, but fulfillment was his real desire. How would he find that?

The hour was getting late and Melk knew tomorrow would be another day of tough physical work in the beautiful spot known as the Majestic Cemetery. He drifted to sleep holding and thinking again about the message in the stone..

Use What You Have; You have what you need; Live in the present to see this.

That night over dinner, Melk reflected on the questions that were floating through his mind, more freely than they had in quite some time.

1. How is it possible that this idea of cemeteries, death and grieving are so foreign to me?

2. Bob mentions that "Nothing Lasts Forever." Is this a good thing or bad thing? What would I do if they did?

3. What can I do from the lessons of Sara to be sure that I remember that life is temporary to make the most of my time?

4. What does it mean that "I have everything that I need?" Do I believe this? What do I feel, if anything is lacking and holding me back in my life? How could I move forward without it?

5. If I focus on my strengths and what I have and using it, what direction would I take my life? What would I do differently today?

6. What is holding me back from doing this?

Chapter Two

Melk learns from his limits.

Melk arrived before scheduled the next day with some aching muscle groups that he had forgotten existed. He had been no stranger to physical work in the past, but this was not the same, and his body was speaking to him. He checked in with Bob and made his way to the shop to prepare the equipment and get a start on the day.

He had not noticed, but Bob followed him out to the shed. As Melk prepared the equipment, Bob asked how it was going.

"How did you enjoy your first day?"

"Well, physically, it was tough."

"Yes, what did you make of that?" Bob asked.

"Oh, it's really no problem. I know it will take a while, but my body will adjust."

Bob nodded, "Funny how physical work can focus the mind."

Melk agreed, thought he knew what Bob meant and headed over to the shed to get work started for the day.

His start was slow at first and then he worked into it. Line trimming was back on the agenda today. It was physically demanding and he could feel it.

"I've been through tough things before," Melk encouraged himself. "Just as in the past, things will get easier as I go along. I'll get more accustomed to it."

This was all the encouragement that Melk needed to keep the morning going. As the sun began to peak out overhead, he felt more than ready for noon, for lunch, for a break.

Lunch was also quiet. He had packed a lunch and was grateful for it, needing the nourishment. He recalled the office jobs that he'd had in the past, where he'd worked and excelled. Often, he'd found many people looking to gab, ready to chat. He had often found that annoying and wondered why everyone did not feel like they had work to do, no time for that. Would he feel differently about that today?

He realized this would not be a concern in the cemetery. Not much chatting seemed to take place. There was a lot that needed to get done. Melk made his way back to the grounds and got started again on the work.

On this, his second afternoon in the cemetery, Melk's mind was active. He started by continuing his efforts to motivate his body through the pain, through the discomfort. Surely his sports experience would help him here. "Look at it as a challenge," he told himself. "Surely, he would come out stronger in the end?"

As the afternoon wore on, his mind became more active and his legs less. He felt himself slowing, his load increasing and his mind racing. Melk was not sure that he was enjoying this or at least his mind poked at him to consider this. What was he doing here in the cemetery? Did he really enjoy this? Did he even look like a cemetery worker? Didn't he have a mighty track record of success in other work locations? How had he arrived here? How long would be here? Where would he go after this? What did it matter?

Melk was carried back to his youth where he had often attended local tractor pull competitions. He remembered how the clean and polished tractors would vent and scream and hiss and pull at the hitch, front ends sometimes coming off the ground as the engines accelerated forward and made progress.

The tractors always pulled easier at first, as the weight on the load remained over the axle. As time and results progressed, the carrying load would start to transfer forward of the axle and become heavier. Eventually, the horsepower would be overcome as the tires began to slow and to sink into the soft ground. At these moments, Melk always felt himself cheering on the decelerating tractor. "Not now, not yet. Keep it up!" he would think.

Each tractor met the same end, some with greater results. What a similarity he now saw in his life- how he had "charged from the gates" as a youth. How he wanted to keep up his momentum and how his tires had bogged down in the soft economy over the past few years. Then he had felt the weight of the load transferring forward past the axle, delivering the final blow, bringing him to a defined stop, accelerating to his end.

As Melk struggled through this analogy, he felt more physical pains, as if he was being attacked on all fronts.

First, it was his thoughts. They closed in and ceased. Then, it was his body. It tightened up as if to make a last effort. Then it stopped.

Melk had reached his limit.

He was brought to his knees with the weight of the physical, mental and emotional assault.

He lay there motionless. Soft soil. Wet grass. No thoughts. Nothing.

Then, it began to rain.

How long did Melk remain on the earth, he was uncertain. Time stood still and he lost track.

He did not feel time.

He did not feel temperature or his surroundings.

He did not feel thought or emotion.

He did not feel worry or guilt.

How much time had passed, Melk was not sure.

He felt the grass press against his hand and skin.

The grass clung to him.

He felt something else. It crept over him slowly at first and then overcame him, with quiet strength. He felt peace. He felt quiet. He felt still. He felt relieved.

Melk felt unaware and yet more in touch than he'd ever been. He found himself in this moment. In the difficultly of this collapse, his mind was focused and silenced. Relieved.

It was endless and yet, at some point, Melk felt a shift.   He felt a lifting from inside himself. He was no longer stuck in the collapsed position. He had never been so low, and yet never felt such an acceleration to rise. And, so he did. He rose to his feet and stood. His spirit rose with along with his legs.

Awareness began to sputter in. His mind began to increase. He quieted it. He had found something peaceful and reassuring in this moment and was not ready to lose it. He rose with a new outlook and moved forward to continue his daily work.

The pain in his legs was less. The pain in his back and shoulders was less. He was able to move forward with less effort. His mind was quiet. The peaceful inner feeling remained.

The end of the day reached Melk with a surprise. Something inside had given him the strength to move forward, to progress. He had felt so broken, that he was not sure what would happen, but an inner strength had brought him back and seemed to be teaching him something.

Melk continued through the afternoon, steadily, without analysis, somehow enjoying his new sense of stillness. He was content to be there, in the moment.

As he made his way back to the shop, he noticed Bob approaching and prepared. Perhaps he had noticed or observed him this afternoon. At first his mind raced and then Melk stopped it, preferring the stillness.

"How's the day wrapping up, Melkior?" Bob asked with a pronunciation that was familiar but off the mark.

Melk nodded at Bob.

"For many, this can be the toughest part of the week. It takes a toll on your body as it works to adjust."

Melk again nodded. "Today was tough Bob, that is true. At one point, I was not sure that I'd make it through. I surprised myself.

Bob looked at him for a moment. This time, he nodded, seemed to understand and paused.

 "How are you doing? Are you finding it easy to stay on task here at the Majestic Cemetery? How are you adjusting?"

"I am not going to say that it was easy," Melk responded and felt relieved as Bob had not mentioned his collapse. Perhaps, he had not observed him. Something told him that he would not bring it up. "The physical work itself allows my mind to focus. Something about it brings about an inner strength. I think that I experienced that today."

"What do you mean, Bob asked?"

As Melk was still working to understand what had happened over the afternoon, his mind carried him back to the conversation with Sara. "Well, I ran into a lady named Sara the other day who told me a lot about her late husband. It does not sound like it was an easy adjustment for her to live without him. Eventually, she was able to do this. Now, she's learned to expect great gifts from the losses that come up in her life. That seems odd to me.

I have been lucky to not have lost any key family members in my life in years. I have not had to deal with that and I'm not sure how I would do. I know that I'll have to deal with this one day, but...

My biggest question is how do you Bob, or any of us work in this environment every day without having it affect our lives? Without having it makes us sad or to grieve other's losses every day. How do we not allow it to wear us out emotionally?"

Bob thought for a minute and looked widely around the cemetery. "It's a beautiful spot, isn't it? Someone put some thought into planning and selecting this place, didn't they?

I truly enjoy coming here every day with the trees and the landscape, the green sloping hills. They are majestic.

You asked about what our families experience every day- the loss and the grieving about how does that effect those of use that work here. How are we not caught up in a constant state of grief or sadness as a result? Is that what you are asking?"

"Yes Bob, that is correct." Melk responded and leaned in closer for the response.

"Melk, I have to say at first, it did bother me. I've been here for many years now and I won't say so much that I've become immune to it, but I've thought more about it. You've probably noticed that our cemetery is a great place for peaceful thought and reflection, haven't you?"

Melk nodded and thought. Sometimes it was peaceful and other times less. Why did he not feel like the same person who had walked through the gates only yesterday? What had changed?

Bob did not seem to notice Melk's deep thought. Or, if he did, he did not respond.

"So, at first I was wrapped up in the grief and loss, the emotion of our families that visit, but the longer that I was here, I noticed that for many there was unquantifiable, unmanageable grief, it did not last forever. It also never went away. But, it did change.

Their visits changed over time, from the early incapacitated visit to the more peaceful, reflective visit.

I've taken some great meaning away with me from this role too. It's a daily reminder that what we have here is dynamic and fleeting and leads to so much more.

It can be so wonderful one day and so challenging the next. In fact, the only guarantee that we have is that it will not be completely the same every day.

Many people forget this. I used to also, but it is a great reminder to not take today for granted.

Since the time that I had my start at the cemetery and today, I've experienced my own personal loss and grief. In many ways, I felt more prepared for it, as much as is possible, when it came to me because of my time here. I am grateful for that.

Many people that I've observed become so consumed by a routine, by a 'busy' life and routine that they don't see how it could ever change or don't take time to think about if it should change. They are really 'along for the ride' until the ride stops or changes direction. They don't take time to step off the assembly line long enough to stick their head up and look around and enjoy the good things in life- beauty, love, grace, acceptance and even the process of change itself."

At this point, Bob, who had not paused from the work he was doing, stopped. He stopped and turned and looked fiercely into Melk's eyes and then, continued.

You must take time to consider happiness and fulfillment in your life. The worst is for many that I've met who are happy or could be happy and never take the time to do it, or even consider it. They wait until a time of loss or a time when something changes and then look around to say, 'Wow, I really was happy then, I just didn't know it.' You can't live like that Melk. Look for and enjoy the happiness in life while it is with you in the present. When it is with you no longer, look for the other points that bring joy and happiness into your life.

These are the things that I've seen, but I'm not sure that I've answered your question directly Melk, so let me get back on task. How do we as professionals in our line of work carry on without being affected?

Well, Melk, my answer to this is that we are affected and we should be grateful for that. We'd be missing a great opportunity if we did not absorb the meaning behind it all. This change is inevitable. Everyone will experience loss in one fashion or another and we should not avoid that. We should use it to remember what is important in life and to think about why we are here.

Each one of us matters and is here to make an impact-to do something that matters. This environment is a great environment to hold up a mirror to ourselves, our beings and our lives to honestly asses our path, our approach and our convictions.

Really, Melk, I am getting ahead of myself. Some of these things may become more apparent to you later in the week, so let me boil my thoughts down to you in this way.

True happiness comes from the inside. We can't attach that happiness to other people or to other things. It starts inside each and every one of us. We need to think about what matters to us, what we are here to accomplish and we need to work towards that end. I believe that the people that we meet and love and associate with along with the worldly goods that many of us put too high of a value on, can augment our experience, our happiness and our fulfillment, but they cannot deliver it.

It is delivered from the inside out. We must be aligned internally and happy internally in order to reflect that and connect with the Who, What, and Whens that interact with us daily. It is more of a choice than we realize. This Majestic Cemetery only magnifies this fact for us and helps us to see it clearly."

Bob took a break, took a deep breath and wide look around the manicured grounds and then continued.

"What do you think about that Melk?"

Melk was definitely thinking about all that Bob had said. The expression on his face made that clear. He stumbled through a, "Yes, I do," and then asked, "How do I know what will make me happy on the inside?"

"Well, that is a tough one, isn't it?" Bob responded. "And, I've already carried on with my thoughts for later into the evening than might be expected. Perhaps, we'll finish up our work and take another look at all of this in the morning?"

Melk nodded.

As Bob was about to leave, he turned briefly to say, "I can tell you one thought that has helped me. Remember what it's like to be a child. Remember what it is like to think clearly about what you like and don't like- what you want to become and don't want to become. Find ways to keep it simple, like we did in our youth."

Melk worked his way out to the Majestic Cemetery grounds to wrap up his work. His body groaned in anticipation.

Melk realized that the break helped him to regain his physical and spiritual strength. He thought of what Bob had said. He talked of reflection on happiness and meaning in our lives and to think simple more youthful thoughts to bring clarity. He talked about how happiness was a choice.

He talked about not associating happiness with other people or objects, realizing that happiness was something generated or initiated from the inside of our beings that radiated out.

Melk was deep in thought and barely noticed a translucent **orange** object near today's path looking over toward him. He moved closer and collected another stone. It read:

Happiness from the inside out

He was not as surprised today, put the stone in his pocket and began to wonder what life was going to look like for him at the end of seven days in the Majestic Cemetery.

Melk began to think about what Bob and he had discussed. He thought about happiness. He thought about how he could tell if he was happy. How could he measure this to be sure?

The last thing that he wanted, as Bob had described, was to miss out on the realization that he is happy until it was gone. So, how would he know? This would require more thought.

Questions that Melk considered:

1. What was it that brought about his collapse?

2. Really, what generated his new life and new energy when at first he thought he had reached an end?

3. Was it natural or not to be at peace with the grieving and experiences that he was experiencing daily?

4. What does it mean to be happy from the inside out? How could he initiate that?

Chapter 3

Melk finds a way to learn from mistakes.

Melk's third day began with an angry wind that blew around anything that was not attached in the cemetery.

Leaves swirled, flags collapsed and garbage, which was one of his regular challenges to control, ran freely through the cemetery grounds. He was quick to get started and noticed his body and equipment starting to work more fluidly together, navigating the stones, working steadily, accomplishing his tasks. This gave Melk more time to think.

As the time had gone on this week so far, Melk had had a chance to encounter daily visitors, spend more time with Bob and ask more questions about the other work taking place in the cemetery. It all seemed rather logical, he thought.

Taking him back a few days, he thought it odd how he had hesitated at the cemetery gate, how he had wondered about what it would be like. He had wondered if it would feel strange- what the work would be like.

As he had learned his work, it actually felt all quite normal, as if part of nature, part of growth, part of the change itself. Why did this surprise him?

Melk had learned from Bob that two funeral services were planned this afternoon in the cemetery. For the Majestic Cemetery, this would be a busy day.

Melk's job would continue much as in the past without change, performing mowing and trimming to have everything well groomed by the time the grieving families arrived. Bob would make the other necessary preparations.

The morning seemed to move quickly today. The sun was nearing overhead when Melk started to feel as he should pick up the pace. He had not completed the entire area that Bob had laid out this morning to be ready for this afternoon. He'd have to be quick.

In his rush, the quality of his work began to slip. He felt he was starting to make up ground as he lost his grip on one of the tools, creating damage to one of the nearby monument stones.

At first, he allowed himself not to notice. He was in a hurry and hurry he would. He focused on completing the work.

Then, as the sun shone from a new direction, the damage was apparent. "Oh," Melk thought, "that's not quite as unnoticeable as I'd thought." His mind began to race, now what?

Well, immediately, it would not matter a great deal. He was gaining ground and would soon complete the agreed upon sections. He was feeling better about that. On the other hand, he should tell someone about the damage that he'd created.

The time for lunch arrived and Melk headed to the shed trying to forget his blunder. He felt himself working to avoid the issue, trying to push away the thoughts and guilt. He did not have to do anything, he tried to tell himself.

He sat down for lunch and was carried back to a time in his early childhood, which he may have forgotten, except that his parents seemed to gain much from the experience themselves and had repeated it as he had grown.

It was an evening and his mom was preparing dinner. His dad was finishing up some work. As his mom cleared the table, moving her purse, something had looked different to her. She examined more closely and found money to be missing from her wallet. This was a surprise and she asked around the family to discover the cause.

Melk had remembered this moment, had been questioned, along with the other family members, had denied everything right up until the end. His mom, as always had persisted and, in the end, found the truth. Melk was the culprit. It had not been easy for him to admit, but he had taken the cash, hoping no one would notice.

His parents consulted and decided that he would be disciplined. Looking back, the most upsetting fact of it all was how his parents had consulted each other, decided the punishment and then let him know what was to be done. "There are some things for which we can protect you, his mom had explained. If you steal, cheat or do things against the law in the world, we won't be able to stop your punishment. And so, we won't this time either. "He could see it coming and it upset him that there was nothing anyone could or would do to stop it.

They had explained this to him and then announced his punishment. He did not recall what they took away or the exact punishment they dealt him, but found that it was really, the slow, steady, unemotional application of that got to him. His mom came to find him later in his room, hiding behind the couch, crying unceasingly and they began to talk.

"How are you doing Melkior?" She asked. He did not answer until she pressed him. Melk had replied, "I just can't get the 'naughties' out. I try, but I just can't." He had remembered wanting to be as good as his Mom and Dad and being frustrated at his failure.

He had believed that his parents and other adults were without fault, without sin, without error. His mom patiently explained to him that was just not the case. Continuously from childhood through adult and all of life, we must all work to make the right decisions, to act with good character, to do what's right and be truthful. It was not easy for him as a child, and it would remain a challenge for him, as it does for all people, his mom included, throughout their life. It was a continuous challenge to do the right thing and make the right choices.

Melk had remembered that point because it really surprised him.

Melk could look back now and understand how this conversation had made him feel better. His expectations had not matched reality. His youthful naiveté had convinced him that he could and should seek to attain perfection as an adult, not realizing that this is not possible on earth. He would have to work every day to do the best that he could. He would also have to realize that those around him to include his family members are working to do the same thing and make some allowances or room for them to do it.

He'd have to learn to forgive the others, as well as himself, as mistakes were made along the way. Owning up to these mistakes he learned could be empowering. Not expecting perfection from himself or from others, made room for mistakes and made it easier to ask for or to give forgiveness. It surprisingly made life easier and made it easier to get along with others.

Some, he had also seen were not able to forgive, but many others had figured this out too and were able. Grace, or "undeserved love" was able to surface during these moments from people who understood that this was not yet a perfect world.

In asking for forgiveness, he was able to feel cleansed and allowed the others involved to feel empowered and good about themselves too. Maybe there were valuable experiences to be gained from all of this, he had thought.

In this situation, he had taken the time to remind himself what was the right thing to do. Own up to the mistake and ask for the forgiveness. Don't hide in the darkness of the error but offer an opportunity for both sides to shine by bringing the failure out into the light.

After the services in the cemetery were completed and Melk had finished owning up to his mistake, describing it to Bob, he emerged from Bob's office feeling refreshed, knowing he had made the right choice. It was just one more opportunity to get the "naughties" out.

Bob was not happy, but had taken the news reasonably well and Melk would do better in the future.

As he walked along preparing to continue his work for the afternoon, Melk noticed a familiar hint of light off to the side of one of the paths. This time it was **red**. Melk moved in that direction and collected a bright embedded stone which read,

Get the "naughties" out; Allow others to do the same.

He wondered more about this place called the Majestic Cemetery and began to look around with greater curiosity. What was the difference between "meant to be and coincidence?" Was destiny an up-until-this-point unknown force that was trying to get his attention? He was not really all that certain.

In a familiar way, Melk deposited this stone in his pocket and continued on his way to finish his work for the day. As he did this, his mind traveled.

The message on the stone was not foreign to him. He did not think of the experience from his youth all that often, but the lesson that it yielded was brought forth in his mind regularly.

Melk knew that he had a hard time with other drivers on the road. He found many of them to be especially challenging. He prided himself in being safe, in following the rules, in working to drive with consideration. Others did not.

They wove in and out and cut him and others off. They held conversations, groomed themselves, did just about everything other than focus on the road, he felt.

It was the message on the stone that really helped him to see this entire situation differently. He realized how many are just doing the best that they can. The expectation of perfection is not realistic. People are people no matter what. We make mistakes. Every day, someone or many are working to "get the naughties out" and he worked daily to remind himself of this, to try to learn to live with grace, offering "undeserved love" in as many directions as possible.

Although Sunday School and church were a sporadic part of his youth, Melk could not help but recall a familiar passage to, "Let he that is without sin cast the first stone." Yes, he thought that makes sense. He might be a wonderful driver, and yet, he had other faults. He had learned to make room for others' imperfections in his life.

As the day wrapped up, Melk worked through a few questions in his mind:

1. What are other examples of times when I expect perfection from others? What can I do in my life to make more room for them to be less than perfect or to make mistakes?

2. How can I work to do the same for myself? When I come up short from my goals, how do I allow room to accept this, learn from it and move on?

3. How do I do better at being more quick and honest about admitting my faults to others, not working to hide them or cover them up?

Chapter 4

Melk learns to help himself.

As Melk rose on the fourth day to arrive at work, his body seemed ready to go. That made him feel good. He was starting to feel as if he'd found a home.

No doubt, as Bob had promised, they'd need him until the end of the week and that would be it. He'd be done and out looking for more work. Where was the value in this he thought? Bob had been up front about all of this at the start he had remembered, making the remark about, "What did he expect, Nothing lasts forever."

Now, Melk was caught in the middle of this thinking. If this only lasts for a week and nothing else lasts forever, then what was the point? Why should he devote himself to the Majestic Cemetery or to any other cause or mission if this was the case?

Now that he was thinking about it, it seemed true too. He could not think of any project or commitment or focus in his life that had ever lasted completely forever.

His family relationships. Yes, he hoped and expected that they would last forever. But, then again he was working in a cemetery, reminding him that even these relationships at a minimum where likely to change before this thing called life was at an end.

His thoughts continued down this path as he made his way to the far side of the cemetery to get a start.

What really was the point? The one thing that would stay constant through this entire experience was he, Melk, himself. He would be in it together with himself and that would not change.

If this is the case, he thought, then I am the only one that is going to be here every step of the way to make sure it matters, to be sure there is a reason and a purpose, to be sure that he had a mission. In this relationship and reasoning with himself, it would make sense to spend some time reflecting, to be sure that his life mattered, to be sure that he was being his own best supporter.

Melk's trimming path today took him more towards the back side of the cemetery. Bob explained that they liked to trim the most heavily trafficked areas of the cemetery closer to the end of the week, to be sure that the most visitors as possible could appreciate their well-manicured appearance over their weekend visits.

He had not spent much time in this part of the cemetery before.
As he rounded a bend in the road, the cemetery opened up to an open area with a large statuesque monument. It was surrounded by flags, moving in the morning breeze, monuments and uniform white grave markers. It was a majestic scene.

Melk reviewed the map again to be sure he was in the right area and moved closer to start his work on the back side of the monument and flagged area with the white grave markers. As he did, he noticed a young man near the back side of the monument, spending time near one of them.

Being careful not to disturb him, Melk moved to the farthest point away and began his work to trim. As he progressed through the morning, Melk monitored the visitor, continuing to give him space, as he did with all cemetery guests.

Nothing seemed to interrupt the visitor's thoughts as he continuously peered down, his hands folded across his lower back, seemingly to be in careful contemplation.

Melk had been in the area for over an hour when the visitor changed his stance, seemed to complete his thoughts and reflections, looking up and around, seeming to once again become a part of his environment, coming back from where ever it was that he had been.

The visitor approached Melk, who carefully turned off his equipment and pleasantly greeted him.

"Good morning," Melk said. The visitor returned the greeting.

"Good morning, How are you getting along this morning? I've not met you in my past visits to the cemetery. Of course, it has been a few weeks. I'm John."

"It is nice to meet you John. I'm Melk. Can I help with anything?"

"Oh, no." John responded, "Thank you. It really is a remarkably beautiful morning at the cemetery, isn't it? I enjoy the sun and the cool breezes. You know, I've met a lot of the people that work here. Are you new to the cemetery?"

"Well, yes, I guess I am. This is day #4. Or, maybe not. As I understand it, no one stays beyond a week. So, maybe I'm becoming an old-timer, "Melk responded with a short smile and then continued, "Really, I am grateful to be here. It is a majestic place. It is really great when you compare it to some of the dark, gloomy office environments in which I've worked. I love the fresh air and the trees, the birds and the breezes. Yes, it is great. Do you come here often?"

John took a step back and responded, "Only as often as I feel the need. I lost a good friend, Mark, who is buried right here, during my time overseas. I come here to remember him, to speak with him, to spend time with him."

"I'm sorry for your loss."

"Thank you." John said and paused.

"We went through some tough times together in combat. We got really close to coming back home together, but not quite, just like the stories that you read in books, you know?

Mark was surprised on his last convoy. We were all surprised. We'd been on so many before. We really thought we'd be spending Christmas together, back home this year. It did not happen. Although, I consider us spending time together now, here.

Neither of us expected to be here forever. I just did not expect to be here without him. Sometimes I feel as if I'm living for two-Living up to my expectations as well as his- my dreams as well as his. Sometimes I feel pressured to do this. Isn't that strange?

I wonder if the roles were reversed, if Mark would feel the same. Probably not. He'd be his active self, his positve self, working to find a way to move on. During our times together, like this morning, I talk with him about things like that."

Melk thought carefully about what to say. He knew John was hurting and grieving. Today, and his life recently, wasn't exactly meeting expectations either, but he did not have to wonder if he'd be home at the end of the year. He did not have to worry about losing close friends in distant lands, out of touch with his family and friends.

"How do you do it? How did Mark do it? What was the reason?"

"Well, we knew signing that we were signing up to be willing to give our lives in the line of duty, in defense of our country. We didn't expect that we'd actually do it.

From day one, it is a 'one day at a time' focus to get through. None of us knew for sure that we'd make it through to meet the requirements to start our new life as military service members, but then, we did. That was just the beginning.

Really, we did not think about it much. We had each other. We went through tough times with each other found ways to give each other a hard time, especially during the tough times. It kinda kept our minds off of everything?

Especially Mark, he wasn't your typical soldier, you know?"

Melk really did not know and just looked at John. "What is a typical soldier?"

"Oh," John responded to his blank look. "As we started out, some just seemed to know. Maybe it was part of their family. Maybe it was a childhood dream. They just knew and would never let on to any doubt. The military was their mission, their life goal- to serve their country, to grow and advance, to make a difference and to make it to 20.

Mark was different. Don't get me wrong. He was motivated. I don't think I've ever seen any one so fiercely focused on accomplishing his goal. He was just more openly considering his goals, was not sure that the military would be a career, a 'lifer' you know, but was so focused on keeping the team together and prepared, on completing this mission. He cared about those around him. He was so easy to get to know. Mark had an easy time making friends."

Melk listened to John and thought. He did not know many who had joined the military or served overseas. He had heard of some neighbor kids from a town nearby that had joined, but couldn't really name anyone today who he kept in touch with in the service.

Mark's story did not quite make sense to Melk, especially after this morning. Mark had not been sure about the military, wasn't planning to make a career out of it. Why had he been so committed to the convoys and to the mission, in countries that Melk was sure that many could not even find on a map. Why?

John seemed again to pick up on Melk's questions. "You know what they say is true. We don't fight for foreign policy or political leaders. Yes, we have to obey the orders, but it's not what keeps us focused on mission, focused on giving more than 100%.

It's really about our team and our shared mission. It's about going through tough times and persevering to the end together; about doing more as a team than we ever thought was possible- more than was possible as individuals, and then wanting to do more.

It is about doing the best that we can with the moment that is given to us. It is not about thinking about all of the other things that we could be doing or about opportunities lost. Combat had a way of making a clear vision for all of us. We did not have time to bog down in over analysis, worry, fear or guilt. It provided clarity.

For Mark and I, we had a strong faith and we knew that things happen for a reason. We knew that we were in that strange, distant country for a reason. We knew that we were in the military for a reason."

"Are you still in.. the military, I mean?" Melk asked.

"Nah," John responded. "I couldn't see that.. I mean, it really did not make sense after Mark was gone. It was something that we'd signed up to do together. It was our shared mission. Now, it is different. My mission has changed."

Melk was not sure what to say. He wanted to thank John for his service, to thank him for his friend, to comment on this strong friendship. He did not.

Instead, Melk's thoughts came back to himself. What was he doing in this cemetery? What was his mission? How would he know? How could he get clarity?

"It sounds like a tough experience. Really, it sounds horrible. Do you regret the decision? I mean the decision to join? Do you regret Mark's decision to join?" Melk asked and then thought maybe he should not have.

Mark straightened up in his stance. He stretched his shoulders back in his frame and paused as if he was thinking. "No, no, I do not. Yes, it was tough. I really wish John was still with me. I miss him every day. I think about it every day. But John and I both believed that things happen for a reason.

It was not a coincidence that we came together as friends and decided to join the military.

"How did you both decide to do that? Melk asked.

"Well, it was easy. We were young. We are still... or, I am still young, but it is an 'older' young, if you know what I mean. I feel like I have a lot more 'life' under my belt.

It was an easy decision then. I believe that youth can have an advantage over age many times in decision making. As I get older, I tend to do more analysis, I am more careful. My decisions tend to be more complicated, but I remind myself that they don't have to be.

When Mark and I made this decision, we were not careless. We were not reckless. We considered our options and thought about them. We talked to each other, decided and then we acted.

We did not regret the decision and yet, we were unsure, not certain to know how to know if we made the right decision."

"But, then, how can you be sure that you did?" Melk asked.

"One thing that I do know is that man needs a mission. A person needs a dream and needs to be working towards something.

If we had not followed our dreams, if we had not acted on them, we would not have had the same experiences, learned the same lessons, and had the same results.

We don't get to choose the time of our passing or elect how much time we'd like to spend on earth, but we do get to control our efforts to make the most of our lives, the most of our experiences.

I know this because through life, and especially through war, I've learned a lot. I've learned to be grateful. I've seen many people and places in much worse conditions than I've had showing gratitude, being thankful for what they have. In those cases, It gave me perspective. It made me grateful. It showed me all of the things that were not missing in my life, something I could not have understood on my own if I had never been there.

It made me think with so many gifts, with so many blessings, what will I do with them? Don't I have an obligation to do something with them?

Do I have an obligation to the others, to my friends who did not come back? This is a question that I've asked myself and continue to do so at times. I feel lucky and grateful to be here. I stop this line of thinking when it gets to the point of making me feel guilty or at least I try to.

At that point, I don't entertain the thought anymore. If I were one of the guys that did not come back and was looking on at all of this chaos from a better place, the last thing I'd want is to make my buddies feel guilt, so I don't entertain it.

My time in the military has taught me a lot. I'm a different person. I'm a better, more grateful person. I've come out the other side as a new person, albeit one who has experienced some tough times. The tough times helped me to become who I am. They forced me to ask these tough questions, to think about what is important and act on it.

My memories and the tough experiences sometimes get a hold of me. I can get caught in re-living them. This is true for many of my buddies, the other 'survivors.' It is the joy and the love that is present in my life that pulls me from the dark memories. It is these thoughts that shine a bright light on top of the dark memories and helps me to get out of the middle of them, not to avoid them, but to move on, to keep living.

I know that I am here for a reason. I am grateful for all that I have. I know that we are not guaranteed a certain amount of time or a certain type of experience and we have to make the most of what we have to gain the best experience.

Despite the difficulties, I know that I made the right decision in joining the military. I listened to my inner still voice and followed my path. I listened to those that I trusted around me at the time. I came out the other end as a better person. This is the mark that shows me that I made the right decision.

Today, I remember this. I need a mission. I won't waste the time or blessings that I carry with me, to include Mark's memory, by wandering through life.

I use what has worked for me in the past. I take all of the information in. I listen to my 'gut.' I listen to my companions. I make a decision. I set a course and I do the best with the daily challenges that come my way as a result- whether it is leading a convoy, or stopping in the cemetery to spend time with my 'old' friend.

Melk, can I tell you one more thing? I know you've got things that you need to get done today too. Just like many people, you've got a 'to-do' list. Having a mission is not all about that 'to-do' list. I used to think that, so I've got to share this.

The to-do list is important. It gets you to where you are today, working in the Majestic Cemetery, but it won't get you everywhere that you need or want to go.

Allow the to-do list to get you to the cemetery. Work to complete your daily tasks to the best of your ability. Be present in the moment. Absorb the meaning of it. Be grateful.

Listen to what life and your experiences are trying to tell you or to show you. Enjoy the message of life in a sunrise or beautiful view. Take time to enjoy the beauty and gifts in your life.

Take time to reflect and listen to your inner, still voice, not the one in your head that goes on and on about what should have happened, what didn't happened, who is better than whom and so forth.

No listen, to the voice deeper down that is helping you to reach your path. It is harder to hear, but it never goes away. In many cases it is an instinct or a feeling. It is easier to ignore in the short term and gets louder as time goes on.

Live to be thankful for what is here now. Look for it. Consider all of the information in your life right now and continuously improve your life mission based on what it is telling you. None of us have to be perfect, we just have to keep trying, making an effort to move forward, to improve.

Have a mission and take time to enjoy the path on which it leads you. Be thankful for this path and for those that you meet and your experiences along the way.

These are the things that I tell myself every day. After going through the toughest times of my life, after losing someone that I cared so much for, I won't take for granted future blessings or wonderful moments and experience. I also won't squander my time here."

Melk thought that he would have to spend some time thinking about this. He thought he could make sense of all of this, but maybe not immediately. Maybe it would take time.

"Can I ask you what your mission is today?" Melk asked thinking; maybe John would not mind sharing this. He seemed to have put some thought into all of this. Melk felt a strong desire to understand, to get to this point of clarity and understanding in his own life.

John answered, "Yes, I would like to share that. When I returned and John was not here, I did not have a choice, I was forced to reflect, to search my soul for understanding, for a new direction, to be sure that my new mission mattered, that it was something that I cared about and could do a good job. What really could matter after all of this?

A good neighbor gave me some advice that I'll always treasure. In order to work through a difficult time.. In order to solve a problem of your own, help others to do the same.

Shift the focus off of you and off of your immediate problem and help others to deal with similar challenges. In any situation, certainly this one, I've been able to find people who have had a more difficult experience and even those who have had an easier go of it. I find value in understanding and trying to help soldiers in both cases. So many times, it is the unknown that is the worst. Our imaginations take over and make it out to be worse than it really is.

This has been life-changing and a big part of my current mission. I help others who have been through a life-altering tragedy gain traction, find meaning, find purpose and identify a mission and plan to move on. It is the driving force that helped me to do the same in my own life and to keep doing it.

It has helped me to realize the blessing in disguise behind all of this. I believe that adversity and conflict enters our life for a reason, to be sure that we don't take our life, our time here on earth for granted.

Adversity, conflict and discomfort drive action. They drive change. They drive engagement. We can be passive about this or we can take an active role.

Taking action is so important. It shifts us from victim to champion and allows us to move forward. Sometimes, we are not certain on what direction or steps to take to move forward, then we must evaluate the options and take the best path. We don't need perfect, just a goal to improve and a willingness to act on it.

Helping others work through challenges similar to our own ensures that we are taking an active role and allow us to see our own situation more clearly.

It makes sure that we are not living our lives on 'auto-pilot,' blending in and moving on. After experiencing tough times, we realize that we have reason to be thankful.

As John spoke, he began to fumble for something in his pocket. Melk, I'd like to you to see something. I'm not much of a writer, but in my quest to help others and in the process myself, I've built somewhat of a summary.

Can I share it with you?

Melk nodded and John handed him a single piece of paper that he could tell had been folded and re-folded many times:

The power of Tough Times, Challenges and Adversity in my Life:

- **Tough times** help us to avoid the status quo, avoid living with binders on, avoiding reality, remembering what that life is dynamic and will continuously change whether we like it or not. Tough times force us to think about what is important to us. Life itself is not the reality, really.

- **Challenges** force us to take an active role in our own life, to take as stand, to care about making a difference, to draw a line between what is acceptable and what is not. Challenges force us to think about who we are as a person, really.

- **Adversity** pushes our back to the wall where we must determine which is the best direction to come out and take action. It allows us the opportunity to develop faith. It forces us out of our comfort zone, to make choices and take action and become better people in the process, really.

Our spirit and soul is the reality that will remain constant into the future. We must listen to it. We must nourish it. We must make time for it. Difficult situations come up in life to give us moments to do just that.

As Melk read briefly over, in not as much detail as he'd like, John continued to talk.

I also find, something I would not have expected as a youth. I experience much greater joy in seeing others succeed than watching myself do the same. The really strange thing to me is that I've succeed and reached goals that I did not think possible, as a result of doing this, by taking the focus off of myself.

When I started off on the mission to help others, knowing that I am not a professional, I was surprised to find that through listening, responding, brainstorming, I could and did help!

Earlier in life, I felt that I could not/ should not 'take my eye off the ball' for even a moment. I felt that doing so would jeopardize my likelihood of success. I now know that setting goals is important, but I must be open to the many different serendipitous ways in which they can be realized and sometimes changed. The connection and desire to help others is directly connected to my ability to help myself.

Melk, this has been a long answer to your short question, but my mission today is to help others get to the 'other side' of their challenging times, including the tragic death of a loved one; to help them to see through it and take action to get through it. In doing so, I'm helping myself to do the same.

I also hope that we will all be better prepared when the next round of challenges come along. We'll all be better prepared and capable to respond.

Melk thanked John and let him know that he would be spending some time thinking about all of this, reading his note. As they said their goodbye's Melk could see John moving out down the path, toward the front gate and exit. He could not help but feel sorry to see him go.

He continued his work through the day and was watching more closely as he trimmed and maneuvered through the stones. As the sun began to crest below the horizon, he notice a blue glint off to the side of this new path. As he picked up the translucent blue stone, he read:

Help others in order to help yourself.

There was a connection with helping other peoples and in the process helping yourself in the long run. What a change when compared to his beliefs of the past, set a goal, determine your mission and work to accomplish it. Why hadn't he been able to see this before?

As Melk sat up that night reviewing the day's events in his head, some questions came to his mind:

1. John had talked about simplifying decision making by looking through youthful eyes. How could I work to do this in my own life?

2. John talked about developing a plan and then allowing serendipity as a force to adjust the plan, being open to the results. This is similar to what has led me today to the Majestic Cemetery. How could I do this in more in my life?

3. How can I help others that are going through similar life transitions as I? How could I reach them and help them to overcome their fears and doubts and take action for the future?

4. What is my mission today? Is it related to my life's purpose? Do I have one? What could I do to develop one?

5. How could I do more to listen to my still, inner voice? How can I differentiate this from the ongoing narration and analysis running within my logical mind?

Chapter 5

Melk moves ahead.

It was Friday for Melk and he felt that he was doing better in his job in the cemetery every day. That felt good.

Melk again found himself wondering what would happen at the end of this work. Where would he find himself? He knew that he was learning a lot, as promised. He valued the experience, was happy to be there, but was not sure of the future path.

He started to review some of the things that he had learned over the week. He had learned about the power of living in the present, about not missing the best time of his life, the most important time of his life by being distracted by the past or the future, places he could not impact.

He understood the importance of this, and yet he kept coming back to the cemetery work. How could he be OK with such limited work, just one week? It was not logical he had thought over and over, from any angle, and yet, it was what it was.

Melk thought about many of the things that he had learned about this week and realized that many of them had to come to him as a surprise. Perhaps, this would also. He decided to act in faith and move forward with the plan as it existed, to believe that it would work out in the end, that it would provide him the experience and knowledge that he required to continue progressing in his life, come what may.

Melk resolved to take it from his mind. He had reviewed it so many times and would review it no longer. He would work in the Majestic Cemetery for as long as they'd have him and then move on from there to find the right next step in his life. He would do this by focusing on and doing the best job that he could possibly do in the present.

Melk realized that life did not offer a blueprint of all of the steps along the road to life. He'd have to work this out on his own.

Melk remembered when he was a child. He had been drawn to math and science in school, leading to his selection to attend a science camp, where he had had a unique experience, related to taking action and determining one's path.

The instructors had presented a magic trick to the class. It involved three ropes of different sizes and resulted in turning the three ropes into equal sizes.

The instructors now asked to find out who could recreate it for them. Who had observed it in great enough detail to be able to do this? A reward was offered for the first student to be able accomplish the trick.

As Melk had observed, a few of the points of the trick seemed to jump out to him, but not all of them.

Despite this fact, something competitive inside of him drove him to raise his hand when the instructor asked who felt they could recreate the magic trick. He just had to try.

At first a sense of doubt, then shock ran through Melk's mind. He wondered, "Who am I to think that I could have figured this out in front of all of these others?" He was talking himself out of it by asking himself what he had gotten himself into.

Then, he silenced his mind and forced himself to get back on task, solving the magic trick and identifying the steps that he was missing.

As Melk stood in front of the group with the three pieces of rope, he worked through his doubts and fears and focused on what he knew, on the steps that were clear to him. He walked the trick all the way up to the threshold and just as he was about to become stuck and stop, the instructor asked, "What is next? Show me your three ropes."

With the pressure of the moment, his intense focus on this specific challenge and his track record of success so far in creating the trick, he was suddenly able to see the step that he had been missing. It was the final method of counting out all of the three pieces of rope, to prove they had been transformed into equal sizes as the audience watched.

In the end, he completed the trick. He was the first to do it in the room and was rewarded with some sort of prize that everyone in the room looked over to view with longing.

The thoughts that came after this accomplishment were what really surprised Melk. As the years had passed since this science camp, he remembered what a thrill this was to achieve the unexpected, to go beyond his limits.

He could not help but think about and ask himself what was it that inspired him to jump up so quickly from his seat, to volunteer to recreate the trick, even when he felt he understood at most, 70% of the steps needed?

He thought more and realized the bigger question would be, what if he had not acted on this? He thought after talking with many of his friends, they did have some idea of how to start the magic trick. They had some idea of where it might go, but they did not take action. They did not jump out of their seats.

Melk realized that what really set him apart and that made a true difference to his success with this magic trick was his desire and ability to take ACTION combined with his vision for success! He realized that he did not need to know all of the answers in life or all of the steps along the path where he'd like to tread. He only needed to know the next step and then to take action to move in that direction as he had done with the magic trick. That is what truly set him apart.

Melk thought more about the results, he thought about his progress at the cemetery. He had learned early on the value of results, on getting things done. Melk was grateful for this. He had seen many who walk around in circles in their lives more than they walked forward, never really gaining a focus on moving forward or getting things done.

Now, Melk thought, where had it gotten him? Why did it matter? He was walking forward, but toward what? He started to resent the cemetery, the system. He began to think. Why, why should I focus on these results? Why focus on these results? What race am I running really? Today, in the cemetery and tomorrow, where? Why commit like this? He did not want to do this anymore. He wanted to move on, to feel appreciated, to feel like there was a future. Maybe he was wrong? Maybe the results were not the most important thing. Did they matter?

This thought rocked Melk to the core. Was he really asking himself this question, something that had always been so important to him? Melk had to take a step back in order to continue. What did he know for sure? If not results, then what?

He thought back in his life. What had delivered to him the best experience? What had been the most rewarding? What had been the most fulfilling? What, from his past, felt the most connected and the most meaningful to his spirit?

This thought, brought him back to results. He knew that these were important to him, but not all results, he now understood.

Certain things and results were important to him and others he could see were not. Wasn't this true with everyone?

Alright, yes, results are important. Certain results were important. Melk liked the feeling of accomplishment every day. He liked the feeling of a hard days' work complete. He liked to know that he mattered. He liked to know that he mattered and people notice the hard work that he completed.

Ok, does this have to happen in the cemetery? No, Melk realized. It did not. He could do this in the cemetery or many other locations. Right now, it was the cemetery and he had to say that he liked this. If tomorrow, it is not, should he be upset? He remembered when he had worked in the gas station and had liked it, did not want it to change and it had. Now, the cemetery was better. What if he had stayed at the gas station?

He'd have to be open to the unknown in the future, to new ideas, to new experiences, he thought. He could see a path of improvement, not always driven by his own action. Sometimes, it was an welcome change and yet, he continuously found himself in better places than he expected.

Melk thought of a time when he felt that he had failed. He had worked hard to become a member of a high performance team and he excelled early.

He was working hard and was getting things done every day. He worked late and arrived early. He felt as if he was valued. It was hectic, high pressured and he knew that few people could operate at the same level as Melk was. His leadership team told him as much.

Then, abruptly, his leadership team was changed. The vision, which had been seamless in the past, was now disjointed, tense and seemed to decline daily. There was a lack of leadership and direction.

Physically and mentally, Melk was struggling to stay connected, to act as if this was work that mattered.   He eventually resigned and felt as this was a failure. He had planned to be a part of this team for the long haul. Before resigning, he had spent time with the team working to reconcile the differences, to build a bridge, with no success.

Now, Melk knew better. He could not cling to a local environment, a local situation, without making room for the future, for other paths and options. He had to be open to life taking its course and to realizing that he was not the only one controlling the outcome.

How could he be so ignorant and think that he had it so well figured out in the past, that he was so powerful as to "make" his life and future on his own? He really had himself programmed to believe hard work, a vision and dedication would be enough to keep him on this course, at the same company, progressing over time.

As he looked back from this time into the future, he realized without the conflict that had come up, without him having the personal courage to be himself and to act in alignment with his own self and beliefs, he would not have found the greener pastures that life had planned.

Results would always be important to him. Maybe he had to be more open to where and how these results were delivered.

If this is the case, could he really be so worried about what the cemetery planned for him? He had to care, he had to work hard, he had to work to move forward, but he also had to understand that life did not offer a blue print of every step along the way. It did not guarantee that anything would last forever. Wouldn't it be unsettling if it did?

These words that Bob had uttered when Melk first started at the Majestic Cemetery were starting to make sense. Without the variety that was added into a plan, he would never be able know his true destiny, to find his true path.

Melk had grown up in an environment where he learned and yearned to avoid conflict and to overcome, to smooth over the conflict.

It was not that he feared it or was not willing to face it, but experience had shown him that it was futile and many times unproductive. Others didn't really want to work through problems anyway, did they? Did he?

For a certain time, he worked to coach himself on how he could have avoided this conflict. Then, he realized, he is not placed here to go with the flow and to always agree. Getting to the point of taking a stand and voicing his convictions was powerful and important.

He no longer regretted it. He realized this had been an example of the adversity that John had mentioned- just enough friction to keep him grounded on his path and open to where it leads.

He knew he could not live into the future anymore thinking that conflict or disagreement was a real problem. He could see the value in handling it proactively with an eye for the future and a belief that it would work out for the best.

> *Faith is what makes up the gap between known next steps and your vision for the future.*

Melk thought through the events, confusion and even turmoil over the past years and realized that it did not matter. Just as the soldier had to go through tough times to find his future and meaning, so do we. What really mattered was what he did with the time called NOW.

He had learned the importance of taking action. Just as the magic trick had taught him not to try to map out the entire course, but to plan to take the next step and the rest becomes apparent over time.

As he was learning to expect his daily message, the brown twinkling light near his shoe and allowed him to read:

Walk forward with a bias toward action.

That's it, he thought. I must make an effort to continuously walk forward. His basketball coach had worked with him on this in the past. He had met with him regularly to talk about goals and results. He remembered the repetitive drills and the goals that at first seemed so far beyond his skill set and then came closer over time.

As he had walked forward in basketball, some days he would make great strides. Other days, he saw a decrease in his skills. His coach had shared with him that this was fine. Human development is not always on a straight, linear path, what was important was a continuous effort. The continuous effort did not guarantee continuous, linear results, but a lack of effort DID guarantee NO results.

Walking forward, Melk thought, was not always easy. For example, he had not been all that excited about getting a start in this cemetery. He had never expected to take on this line of work. It was his bias towards action and desire to walk forward that had brought him through the gate that morning and now, had carried him through almost the entire week.

Now that the week was nearing an end, this same skill would carry him out the gate and ensure that he would survive and even, get back on top of his life. His track record here and this thought gave Melk a boost in energy and confidence. He had not thought for a long time about how many strengths and blessings he really had and it made him feel grateful and content.

It was funny to him how so many of the lessons that he was learning this week were starting to overlap and support each other, how they were allowing his mind to think more clearly and to see a path to the future (housed in a clear focus on the present) that he had not been able to see before.

As Melk was wrapping up, Bob walked over.

"Good afternoon Melk, How did things go today?"

Melk thought for a moment to consider the question. "Fine," Melk answered. He was not always sure what Bob wanted to hear as an answer to this question.

Did he want to know how the work had progressed? Did he want to hear about families who had visited the grounds, or was he more interested in Melk as a person?

Melk always chose the simple answer. The work went well and he was really feeling great about his accomplishments. He could look back at the end of the day and see the results. The grounds looked great because he was there. He had made a difference.

"Can you come in earlier tomorrow?" Bob asked. It's Majestic Cemetery Celebration Day and we've got some items to complete that we weren't able to get done today.

Melk had noticed some additional tents and equipment being set up today, but had not had time to ask.

"Sure," he answered.

"Great, Let's meet up at the office tomorrow and we'll go over what needs to be done. The celebration starts early afternoon, so we'll have plenty of time to get this wrapped up."

As Melk headed home, he wondered what was included in a Majestic Cemetery Celebration. How unique, he thought to hold this in a cemetery-unique or maybe more like strange.

Over the past few days, he had learned that a cemetery was much different than what he had at first expected. But, a ground for celebration, he was not sure. This could be interesting. He was every day realizing that things are not always what he had seen in the past- that he had more to learn. He was welcoming that more and more every day.

That night, Melk had more questions running through his head.

1. What is the value of a "bias toward action?" What drew that out of me at the science camp? How can I find ways to do this more in the future?

2. How do I really feel about conflict? In the past, I've worked to avoid it and now can see how it can be a healthy catalyst (another form of John's adversity) to reach a better place and to grow. How will I know one from the other?

3. If in life as in sports, some days I can expect great growth and less on other days, how will I know when I have a problem, when I am not on track to continuously improve?

4. How can I help others to jump from their seats to take action and move forward?

Chapter 6

A Majestic Celebration comes to the cemetery!

Trees were adorned with vivid decorations. Colorful windsocks greeted visitors at the entrance. A stadium stage was erected at the central part of the cemetery and refreshment stands as well as discrete trash receptacles were place at regular intervals around the grounds. Additional benches were scattered throughout. It was clear that a large crowd was expected.

Musicians were setting up equipment on and near a stage by the front gate. Balloons of all sizes and colors were dancing in the wind at many places on the grounds. New floral arrangements were visible from beyond the gate. As Melk arrived, he was surprised, the grounds had truly been transformed. He went to meet Bob.

Bob was outside the shed, working to troubleshoot a problem that had had come up with one of the tractors while distributing equipment and decorations throughout the grounds.

Melk approached him, still carrying his look of amazement on his face. "Everything looks so festive and great. What happened?"

"That doesn't say much for what we do every day," said Bob with a smile.

"No, I mean, it really looks lively today. I was trying to visualize or have an idea of what to expect today and I was pretty far off target."

"What did you expect?" Bob asked.

"Well, for one thing. No balloons. I've seen them before at many parties, but this isn't a… I mean, we don't have parties at cemeteries, do we?"

"This is the twelfth year in a row that we've had this party at the Majestic Cemetery. The town seems to like it. The numbers grow a bit every year.

We've come to know it as a celebration, which I'd say, yes, it is the same as a party."

"How can that be? Weren't the families upset? Didn't they think of it as… well, disrespectful?

Bob turned to look at Melk as he said, "Yes, it is true that some were surprised, weren't expecting it. Some were critical, but many more were excited.   In the end," Bob said, "Cemeteries are for the living. They are here to help the grieving to remember, to go on living and to celebrate life where they can. We spend 364 days of the year in more or less quiet remembrance and we've chosen this day to host a celebration, to invite the community to the cemetery and to help them remember their loved ones, while remembering the joy in their life.

Many did not come the first year. More began to come on the second and third year. This year, I expect most of the families will be here. I think they've put some thought into it and realized that it is a good thing to remember their loved ones in this joyful way, and so they do.

Many have said that's their family member would have wanted after all, not a stuffy, closed up sad event, but an open-air, vibrant celebration.

"In fact, after working in a cemetery for so many years, Melk, I can tell you that that is one of the greatest misconceptions. Many people think similarly at first and it goes something like this…

> *When I pass away, I don't want you to do anything fancy or expensive. You can cremate me and then I don't care. I don't want to be a lot of bother or trouble. I want to make it low cost and easy for you to move on.*

"It sounds selfless at first, doesn't it, but this thought process conflicts with itself.

The fact of it is, Melk, these people have never really thought this through. They have not thought about what it will be like when they are gone. It is not about 'what they want' at that point, but more about helping their loved ones to go on with their lives, to find meaning and routine and joy.

They must learn to live anew in peace with the gap that's been created when their loved on departed.

Yes, it may be cheaper and seem simpler, but they have not factored in the grief process, the process of saying goodbye for now.

Many people, especially as they age, may feel as if they are 'ready to go' and assume that everyone else is ready for them to do the same. For older family members, when they were able to see it coming, right down to the youngsters whose passings were tragic. I've seen some of the best healing take place in the cemetery.

There must be something to gathering as a group, saying goodbye, talking, crying, laughing, sharing stories and experiencing it together, because these families seem to have it 'more together' in the end.

I'm not sure that you've had the chance to witness this Melk while you've been with us, but some of the toughest times are had by the families, widows or widowers who try to hold on to their loss, who are not willing to face reality.

They will chose to cremate their loved one and place them in an urn. Then, they will carry that urn along with them where every they go- in the car, watching TV, etc. They live their life making believe that they are still with them. Sure, they are there in spirit and they will stay with them in spirit in a new way.

I've seen these same families come back to the cemeteries months or even years later and decide to finally put their loved ones to rest. At that point, they're forced to re-live the loss, to experience it anew.

Over the time that has passed, these same family members, rather than processing the loss at a funeral or committal service have been forced to piece meal the experience in the most unexpected and uncontrolled way.

They'll run into a neighbor or a cousin at the grocery store one day and get to exchange memories and condolences there. The next day they'll run into Uncle Charlie at the school and re-live it again and so on and on.

You can see, Melk, how the best intentions to keep things simple and un-costly can actually have the opposite experience, turning the experience into a very tough, extended and un-healthy grieving process for their loved ones.

Rather than being able process the loss and the grief and begin the transition to a new life, they are forced to live in the middle of their loss, the worst part of it for months or years on end, making it tougher on everyone.

There is really something to be said about a family and community gathering together at the cemetery to say their good byes, not to forget, but to share and learn to live after the shared loss.

For example, you met the Master family that owns the garage down the way, I believe you said?"

Melk nodded.

Late last year when their grandfather passed away, many could see that he was ready to go, had been for some time. Old Man Master would have told you that himself over the last few years. He became rather bitter as his time grew short, actually keeping many loved ones away. But, do you know, at his funeral, he had more cars here than I can remember in some time.

His passing and service at the cemetery really brought the community together. Many were there to remember how he had touched him through his many years in this town. It was powerful too with this group of over 200 people all together sad and at the same time happy, sharing stories of grief and remembrance. It was really something to see. Over the recent months, groups and sometimes individuals continue to visit, continued to share stories, continued to find their own way to 'let go' and move on.

They shared stories with each other that many had not known. Ms. Clara let his children know how grateful she was for helping her out of a sticky situation as she had run out of gas on the road one day with her young family.

She said she was so embarrassed, never thought it would happen to her, but he helped so graciously, never asked for anything in return, and then, much to Ms. Clara's relief never said a word about it to anyone.

Then, the Clarke family shared that after Mr. Masters' children had grown up and moved out of town, he'd helped their boys build the grandest float for the town parade that anyone had ever seen. The fire hose actually worked!

The Masters children are grown up themselves now with their own children. It's something that they'll never forget and enjoy talking about even to this day."

"So will we see many families such as this today, while at the Majestic Celebration?" Melk asked.

Bob turned out his palms and said. "Yes, most certainly you will see them. And, they won't be difficult to spot. At the end of the day, you will feel good about their visit, glad that they were here. It will add to your knowing that what you did today, this week, mattered.

There will be another group that will also catch your attention and make you think. Every year at least one group comes up to tell me how they wish they had more family members to visit. Someone is missing for them here at the cemetery.

They share their experience grieving for the family member in isolation. Everyone should have a place to be remembered.

Just last year, a lady came to the celebration from our neighboring town. Yes, she had family to visit and seemed to enjoy her time with them. Then she came to me and seemed to be looking for someone to talk to.

She told me of her Great Aunt who had passed away. She went on and on about what a great lady she was, but what stuck with me was her sorrow. It seemed that her Aunt made it an annual priority to remember everyone's birthdays. Everyone, including this niece received a phone call, a gift or something in remembrance.

After her passing, this young lady really wanted to able to do something for her as her birthday approached. Unfortunately, she found no way to connect with her, to plant flowers or to be with her. She was un-reachable in an urn on her distant family member's mantle. The living room did not seem like the right place for her to grieve or to connect. She longed for a way to do this, to find peace and some sort of closure.

"I was not expecting this," Melk thought, but he could see how grieving might include many different stages and emotions, the value of gathering the community together to say goodbye as a group and the joy, sorrow, gratitude and more that would be experienced.

He also thought about how this cemetery was allowing him to see the world from a different light, a new perspective and a new reality. He never expected that, but somehow, he appreciated it.

Bob and Melk worked continuously to set up the chairs, to tie in with the sound and stage crew, to place additional balloons and to rehearse the paths the shuttle car would take to assist anyone who needed it as the people made their way into the heart of the cemetery and into the heart of the celebration.

One of the areas that required their attention was an outdoor screen placed near the central office. One of the power outlets had not been working as needed. Bob and Melk replaced it with one that worked. As they ran the line, Melk could see a preview of the expressive videos, quotes, music and photos that would be run on this screen.

They were so focused on life and experiences. They were so focused on joy and expressive memories. One video showed a small boy, must have been seven or eight or so running, playing with friends, laughing and then rolling on the open ground of an open field with friends and family- more laughter and joy.

A large furry dog- maybe a retriever pranced nearby as a seamless member of the family. Melk could see how there was beauty in a good life well remembered. There must be something to that human part of grieving and healing together as a community, as a family- something that could not be re-created as an individual, could not be outsourced to another time or place.

As the set up near completion and lunch was complete, Melk made his way to the front entrance to join the team that would be directing traffic. The Majestic Celebration would kick off with a program of entertainment, music and a message from a community leader.

Each year had a different theme, Melk learned. This year, a message would be shared with participants on genealogy. One local family would share their experience and process for connecting their family tree with loved ones buried in the Majestic Cemetery, as well as other local cemetery grounds. They had also found and mapped ancestral ties back to old Europe and a cemetery there.

Bob explained that throughout the year, they received many calls on the subject and requests for digital photos to be sent. He could tell from the volume that families' interests were growing in this area and it would be of interest to many of the families in attendance.

Most families would arrive at the start to catch this celebration and then, spend the remaining part of the day, walking the grounds, enjoying music and food, as well as a memorable family picnic. A tour would also be offered, giving highlights of the famous cemetery residents as well as highlights of the historic cemetery grounds.

The cars started to pour in right on schedule. Melk guided them to the parking areas, one after the other, snaking around, filling the grounds. It was clear that they were there to enjoy themselves. No heavy hearts, no weighted souls, just car loads of people preparing for the experience.

They must have attended in past years, Melk thought. They all seemed comfortable and seemed to have an idea of where they were going.

As the traffic processed, the band was ready to great them at the front gate. He was more than curious to see what was planned as a part of the celebration.

Would there be somber, eerie strings serenades?. Or, maybe an longing tuba? Perhaps, one of the veterans' bands would join to play songs from eras gone by?

The musicians started out with a musical tribute that spanned past eras and then began a modern and festive combination. It included many types of music with different tempos, genres and beats. It all seemed to flow very well together, where the diversity brought out the strengths of the different selections within the collection.

As Melk observed a break in the program, a familiar face emerged from the crowd. It was Ms. Sara from his first day on the job. She was not fast, but definitely energetic on her feet.

She came over to Melk. "And how's our newest Majestic member?" Then, other visitors from the week came over to visit. It was like a reunion and Melk found himself reviewing the lessons of the week.

Lesson One: *Use what you have. You have all that you need. Live in the present to see this.*

Lesson Two: *Happiness from the inside out.*

Lesson Three: *Get the "naughties" out; Allow others to do the same*.

Lesson Four: *Help others in order to help yourself.*

Lesson Five: *Walk forward with a bias toward action.*

Lesson Six: *See the party!*

Melk thought that he saw many like her within the crowd. Many who seemed happy to be there, with joy and purpose.

He could not say that he saw this was true for al. Instead, he noticed one lady who seemed out of sorts. She was consulting with one of the staffed team leaders, perhaps making a request. Melk observed and thought, based on her body language that he was relieved to not be on the other end of that conversation.

As the break in music and the program continued, Melk watched this women move from the one team leader and then on to another near the office, making unsatisfied unsettled gestures. Her level of irritation seemed to be growing, along with the color of her face.

He thought to himself, "Surely, everyone must have an off day from time to time." But how many have I seen in the past who have a continuous series of off days, a trend you might say.

Melk thought back to the church where he had grown up. Off and on, mostly on, his parents would take him to different programs, Sunday school and other events at the local 4-H and within the community. As he grew up in the community. He now remembered the ladies- the ladies that were the pillars in this church and community groups.

Yes, many, most, he thought, were joyful and worked and rejoiced regularly there. They worked hard too. A couple of those smiling faces seemed like remote family members to Melk, just a great joy to be around. Even as a child he could see this and recognize that not all of the ladies had the same approach.

There were others. They were well respected too and worked hard. He knew that. Involved in everything as he recalled, they definitely worked hard.

Somehow, it did not bring them the joy that it brought the others.   He remembered the to do lists and them ushering the group from one place to another, working through what needed to be done. Just like the other group of ladies, they certainly got a lot done, however, they did not seem to enjoy it. In return, Melk remembered not enjoying it either. Then, he realized that maybe they did not want to be there either.

How could this have been, Melk thought. This was a congregation, a group that he remembered hosting joyous celebrations, a lot like today. Why weren't they a part of the festivities.

Just like the lady that he was watching today, why did they not see the joy? As he looked around, he was starting to expect this every day now, a pink glimmer came from behind an edged path. He picked it up and it read:

See the party!

Well, isn't that true, Melk thought. So many were not able to see the bright side of the celebration, to be thankful for the wonderful elements.

He thought of the church ladies again and saw the similarities. It is great to be focused on getting things done. It's great to feel a connection or even an obligation to a group to serve and get the work done, but when that connection takes you out of touch with your inner self so much so that you are unpleasant and don't want to be there, it's problem.

Just as Melk watched this group that could not see the celebration, could not see the balloons, the church ladies had lost their joy.

Wow, what a loss, as if they've become blind to the joy in life. They've lost the daily gratitude for the blessings that brings joy. Without this, it is as if they are going through life with blinders on, taking it for granted, not remembering that it is not forever and will be gone one day. He thought about how he could apply this to his life.

Melk had to admit that he had not been all that grateful through this transition that he was currently experiencing. In fact, he had not been all that joyful either. He could see how he, himself should learn from this experience and others throughout the week. Melk must take the time to remove his blinders, to be aware of the blessings and wonderful experiences of the present moment and not get caught up in the to do lists of the world.

He thought of the small things that were not so small. He thought of his gratitude for being here, for the inevitability of knowing that one day he would not and the benefit of realizing this.

He thought of his health, of the amazing miracles that he was barely able to comprehend taking place every day in his body, his muscles, his cells, on the earth. How self-centered he had been to take this gift for granted.

He thought of the first day when he entered this cemetery and saw the beauty, saw the rainbow, saw the life. It was remarkable and if he had had his head down the entire time, he would never have noticed.

Melk thought of the lady who continued to grieve her husband with joy and gratefulness, how she had found peace and learned from the experience.

He thought of Bob and all the lessons he seemed to pick up from his many days working here in the cemetery, how he was for this. What would bring other to this same valuable perspective? Wouldn't it help them if they could only see this?

Melk remembered the day when he was brought to his knees, how it was difficult and so simple all at once. He remembered the feeling of peace that overcame him as something from the inside and outside allowed him to re-group, to rise back to his feet and see clearly that his life would be different and he would be OK, ready, even excited for this.

He thought of the simplicity and clarity that was presented to him after he "hit bottom" and collapsed and how it helped him, from the inside, to discover the path that would help him to climb out.

Melk had realized through much of this that he was in the cemetery because he chose to be. He had asked to be there and the longer he went along in the week, the more he felt that he was there for a reason. He was there for the experience. He was there to create an experience. He was there to help others in a job that mattered, and brought joy.

He thought of Mark and the military veterans, working to find their new way in life. He thought of his struggle between reconciling his memories of his friend, of combat, of suffering and how he works to bring that to a joyful perspective today, honoring and working to peacefully remember his buddies who did not make it home, while helping others and finding purpose and meaning in his own life.

He thought, that is a big difference when compared with others who were in places, in jobs, in situations because they felt obligation instead of out of choice or inspiration and never took time to consider their choices, or listen for their inner voice and inspiration. He realized how important it really was to do this. Those who are not able, don't only hurt themselves, but also those around them.

Melk thought of the times when he had worked in a role because he felt obligated vs. inspired. He thought of the core difference in approach to getting the work done, the core difference in completing the job. These two situations brought about very different emotions and motivations within in him down to his soul.

There really is no other choice between misery or taking risks, moving out of your comfort zone to follow your path to reach your destiny. Where much of the week, his job had seemed strange to him, now it was different. Now, with his new perspective and fresh set of eyes, it made sense!

He was looking from the inside out, rather than the outside in as he had in the past and It made sense.

As the celebration continued, Melk watched the people move in and out of the cemetery grounds, some with joyful emotions, some with strife, some with no emotion at all, not really seeming to be there at all, wandering.

He realized that would always be the case and he was thankful to have the eyes opened up to see the difference, to be the difference.

He saw the music continue and the son move from east to west and the shadows alongside the monuments.

Another rainbow came and went. Some noticed and some did not.

Overall, Melk was surprised. The group seemed generally joyful. They seemed to be enjoying their time. Melk enjoyed this. Yes, joy could co-exist with grief, sorrow and departure.

Melk felt good. He felt confident. He was one who could see the party. He could see the celebration. With the celebration, he lost focus on the work that was being done, that he was doing. It was getting done, but Melk was consumed by the party going on around him and being surrounded by the festive celebration.

He realized the choices presented.

One could learn to work through the party or party through the work. Both had very different meaning internally to each person. He was thankful to be able to see the difference and make a choice to be happy.

Melk realized that these different approaches to life would always be present. People would always look differently at life. Difficult people would always be there and it was his choice how he'd handle them and work with them.

As Melk walked home that afternoon, he received a call that his auto repairs were nearing completion. He may be wrapping up his work tomorrow and be ready to be back on the road all at the same time… better than he could have arranged if he had planned it himself, he thought.

Again, the questions began to arise in his head.

1. As I've changed over the past few days, I see how my life is different when I'm able to **See the party** while doing the same work that I'd done earlier. Why does it feel so different to me now?

2. A party environment with balloons and people and music draws the joy from one's spirit, activating it. How can I create this same experience for myself daily with an internal focus that allows me to have the same type of experience daily?

3. What can I do to help others See the party and experience joy and happiness from the inside?

4. What really is the difference in acting or working out of inspiration vs. obligation? How can I create more inspired moments in my life?

Chapter 7:

The river runs into obstacles and yet sticks to its course.

As Melk showed up for his final day at the Majestic Cemetery, he felt prepared. He had learned so much from his time on the grounds that he knew he would never find himself in such a tough spot in the future.

His new approach would ensure him a sound footing on which to grow and prosper.

As he approached the shop and found Bob, he was surprised to see him dressed in unique attire. Bob was wearing his Sunday best and did not at all seem ready to work.

"Good morning Melk, How are you doing today," Bob asked.

"Great," Melk answered. He was happy to be there and excited to put to work the lessons that he'd learned. "I've learned a lot this week."

"I'm happy to hear that Melk. You've done great work for us here and I appreciate it. We won't be working today, as it is a Holy day, a day of rest.

Melk nodded as Bob continued.

"I've prepared your final paycheck." And he handed it to Melk.

"I wanted to share one final thought with you before you go. I think our work in the cemetery can leave you with an internal strength and solitary focus. It can really help you to sort things out in your mind and give you a great perspective on your life. Have you experienced any of that while you were here?"

Melk thought back to all of his lessons on moving forward and motivation, finding happiness and helping others to help himself and nodded in agreement.

"This is great," Bob said, but there is another perspective to consider, a very important one, especially today.

We are not alone here in this condition. God is love, God is alive and God is all around us.

It is another benefit of the job that we do to help others through these tough times. As we do it, we can see that He is present to carry families through these tough times and get them to the other side. Others never get to see this until they are on top of it.

I bring this up now because, although the cemetery may have bared its secrets to you this week, I don't want you to leave thinking you've found everything that you need as an individual to move forward, to prosper and grow like I know that you will do.

The item that is missing is Faith and Awareness of God and a desire to continue to progress along your spiritual path. If you can combine this with all that you have learned this week, then you will be ready.

Melk nodded in agreement, feeling that he was ready. He had not spent much time in spiritual development over the past few years, but this week had brought him much closer to God, to remind him that there was more than what meets the eyes in everyday life and to embrace it.

Melk was grateful for his time here at the Majestic Cemetery and for the people he'd met and lessons he'd learned along the way. He was anxious to put it to work.

As Melk made his way back to the front gate, he had to admit that his eyes were searching. As he neared the front gate, he could not miss the shining **yellow** stone as it read:

> *Faith like a river.*

He would take this stone with him on his new journey that starts today. He would use it to bridge the gap between understanding the next couple of steps and his final vision, his final destination.

A river flows and bends. It rolls through tough terrain and beautiful landscapes without a delay, working through the obstacles on its path. It stays its course without knowing exactly what lies around the bend, knowing that it will reach its final destination at just the right time. It does not need to worry or fret or fear or analyze, simply focus on and do the best it can to manage the path that is laid out in front of it, the path that has been prepared for today. The rest will be taken care of in time.

This stone would be at Melkior's side to carry him through the tough times, the quiet times, the times that he knew would come up- when he'd have to take two steps backward to be prepared to take a step forward. It would be his guiding light. It would shine inside of him and he would take it out, make it visible to others within the world as a model for them to see.

Melk understood that although the happiness and desires and motivations had to start from the inside, that once had these items were in alignment, he was ready to engage a much more powerful all-encompassing force; the force of Faith and the strength of knowing that he was not in this alone. He was never alone.

He stepped outside the gates of the Majestic Cemetery without looking back. He stepped forward in Faith, knowing that he had a plan, he had a vision, but somehow things never worked out exactly as he had expected. In fact, they usually worked out better than he had expected in the long run and better than he had planned on his own.

He was excited to see what next adventure awaited him around the corner, up a head, knowing God would help him to navigate it and help him to come out on top.

I wish you these same results as you start off on your journey outside the gates of the Majestic Cemetery!

Afterword:

People are busy. Organizations are stretched. Schedules, planners and online calendars are full. Regularly, people and organizations are asked to do more with less. The importance of results and continuous improvement is certain, but we know that to live a fulfilled and meaningful life, we must remember that it is about more than just work and income. It is about connecting professional accomplishment with meaning, but we are not always sure how to fit it in, to balance it all.

This is a big topic that could take a complicated approach. For you that know me, you know that's not for me. I believe that the best approach is the simplest. Of course, the toughest part can be to find it.

Our greatest challenges in moving forward or planning is usually ourselves. To break through these tough times, think on a simpler level. What's the one thing that I need to do right now to move forward? What's the next step? Small steps over time add up to big progress. We must be aware of our goals and our vision, our desired direction in order to do this. We must have spent time envisioning and mapping them out.

The toughest part of improving our companies, our organizations, our lives or our situation in life is to **take the time** to think about what is important to us, what is our vision for improvement and connectiong to meaning and then take the next small or large or even lateral step in the path to attaining that goal.

The second, slightly more complicated step is to ask, "Am I on the right path? How do or will I know?" Part of our mission is to determine when our work in one focus area is done and when it is time to change and focus on a new area. I've heard it said that the enemy of "good" is "perfection." I agree.

Sometimes we can select these changes of focus. Others times, life forces these decisions and changes upon us. Sometimes we delay, postpone or hesitate. Either way, it is our time to change and our time to grow. As an organization or as an individual, if we do not listen to our inner voice or respond to the change that life is throwing at us, our growth and development will stagnate.

I've had the great fortune in life to be exposed to a lot of diversity- in people, in organizations, in work environments and industries. I've learned a lot from these opportunities. From all of these, my time working in cemeteries stands out.

Cemeteries are beautiful and peaceful. They are vast and open. They are joyous and heartbreaking. They are quiet and powerful and very realistic. They remind us to every day to keep the end in mind, to remember that each one of our journeys has an end. With the end in mind and with no guarantee of when it will arrive, we find great opportunity in the thought process and conclusions that are presented. It is very difficult to avoid reality in a cemetery, although some manage to do so.

Life is short for all of us in the end- whether we wander through aimlessly or plan and direct our steps and continuously improve towards our goal. Do we search for meaning along the way or simply go with the flow? I find it ironic that the reality, beauty, peace and power of the cemetery forces us to re-think our previous reality. It forces us to evolve.

Whether we are at the cemetery for a visit, there to grieve or there to support others, when we leave we feel a shift in our own reality.

This shift in reality is what this story is all about. It is an opportunity, if we are able see it as such- an opportunity to re-cast or adjust our lives around the "real" realistic principles that matter to us all in life.

I am grateful for our time spent together in the Majestic Cemetery and welcome your thoughts, comments, questions and feedback at www.findyourfantastic.com or email at marceaweiss@gmail.com

Thank you!

www.ingramcontent.com/pod-product-compliance
Lightning Source LLC
LaVergne TN
LVHW061336060426
835511LV00014B/1954